You Might Need A Bigger Hammer

By

Paul Richmond

Published by Human Error Publishing
Paul Richmond
www.humanerrorpublishing.com
paul@humanerrorpublishing.com

Copyright © 2015
by Paul Richmond
All Rights Reserved

ISBN:
978-0-9833344-3-9

Front Cover:
Paul Richmond

Back Cover:
Paul Richmond

Human Error Publishing asks that no part of this publication be reproduced or transmitted in any form or by any means electronic or mechanical, including photocopy, recording or information storage or retrieval system without permission in writing from Human Error Publishing. The reasons for this are to help support the artist.

A Professional	8
Not Impressed	10
4891	11
Our Ancestors	12
Am I Going To Die Soon	13
I Have A Father Like You	15
It's Snowing and Cold, May 2011	17
Looking In a Window Of A Cafe	18
The Light Turned Green	19
Northampton - What About the Artists?	21
Smoochie Mochie	23
Snow Shovel	24
Taken	25
The Dalai Lama	26
Tooth Fairy	28
Near The End	30
Pushing Back and Forth	31
Use Titanium	33
Money In Different Sizes	35

Defending The Elves	36
Don't Eat The Yellow Snow - Thanks Frank Zappa	39
You Have Such Cold Hands	43
I Love the Photo	45
She's Suspicions	47
Valentine - Cupid	48
What Can I Say	51
Watch This	52
Her Biggest Fear	54
Self Awareness Sections	55
Searching	59
In The Good Old Days	60
What Did I Just See	62
More Material	64
The Look	67
Let The Negotiations Begin	68
It Occurred To Me	69
Now I Know	71
I Need The Money	74

Homeless	76
Pep Talk	78
Can't Wait For Summer	80
The Best Friend	81
Rocks	82
Let's Be Clear	83
The Pope & The Dog	84
If You Are Going To Remember Anything	85
Who's Your Captain	86
The Story Survived	89
Garlic	90
Save Grandma	92
Published Poems	97
Paul Richmond	99
Reviews	100

A Professional

3 nuts and bolts
Needed to come off
To remove the broken part
Seems simple enough
Unless you don't know which wrench to use
Or
The nuts and bolts just won't come off

I knew which wrench to use

1,2,3
I'd have those bolts off
New part back on
Be on my way

I couldn't get them to budge
No matter how much I moaned and groaned

I soaked them
With WD 40
Nothing

I heated them up
Nothing

I put an extension on the wrench
For more leverage
Nothing

They wouldn't budge
I couldn't get them off
I finally surrendered
It's time to take it to a professional

I watched the professional closely
Trying everything I had
With no results.

Watching the professional
Having the same problems
Was satisfying

I noticed the professional always carried a hammer
In between the various steps of soaking and heating
The professional would give the bolts a few taps
And try each step again
Nothing
After the extension on the wrench was tried
Along with tapping the bolt with the hammer
The professional went into the back room
Coming out with a very large hammer
Whack
Smashing the bolts into tiny pieces
The part flew off

I looked on in disbelief
I learned that day
Sometimes you just need to use
A bigger hammer

Not Impressed

At a party
The conversation was more about impressing
Rather then getting to know each other

People talking about their heritage
Their families coming over on the Mayflower
Talking about their relatives being great artists
Stating their gene pool superiority

As far as I know
Half of the people who came on the Mayflower
Died in the first winter
I question creativity being a guaranteed gene

When it was my turn
I said
My family has a long history
Of being optimistic
Since my first relatives
Came over on the Titanic

Grandpa is credited
For the family's appreciation of theater
For none of us would be here
If he hadn't put on such an amazing performance
In the life boat
As a woman

They weren't impressed

4891

4891
Can you hear the drumming
There is always drumming
Chanting
Thousands of years
Millions of years
People
Drumming and chanting

As the story goes
There is always a ranking system
Who's on the bottom
Who's on the top
Those on the bottom
Are drumming
Banging on anything they can
Get their hands on
Shamanistic rituals

Their voices
Chanting
Loud and clear

Asking
Asking that the violence stops
Asking to be treated with respect
Asking that the destruction stops
Asking to give up the idea that you are in control
Living with nature
Not trying to control it

Our Ancestors

I am not talking about Uncle Ray
Who lived in Buffalo
Who had a huge belly

No I am talking about Uncle Yezu
Who lived on a different continent
At a different time

Both the continent and Uncle Yezu
Are long gone

I am talking a long time ago
But who remembers that

Am I Going To Die Soon?

Yes it could be any moment
Any day
Just like that
Everything is left the way it is

Look at this mess
Whatever I was saving this or that for
It all lives in the dumpster now

And what did I think
I was doing with my life
Was there a purpose?
Did I fulfill it?

If there are any judgment gates
The defense
Will be
I had followed my inner voice

Some warned
I could be listening to the wrong voice
Especially if I am hearing more than one
I am told to seek help

I just felt a pain in my chest
Does that mean it's over
It seems
I am still capable
Of making purchases

And I am still pressing numbers
That led me through menus
While I wait on hold

I anticipate the answer
To my question
Finally I get through
To a live person

I ask
Am I going to die soon?
I am told when I least expect it
And if I don't try to kill myself
I'll die when it's my time

I Have A Father Like You

My father is going to be 89
He has always loved making deals
Getting good deals
Is what life is all about

He can still get around
He still drives
The tire tracks across the front lawn
No one seems to question

He drives to a few different stores
When he's out shopping for food
In order to take advantaged of the deals

As the story goes
He went to an Aldis
Who now was taking credit cards
So he remembers pulling out his cards to pay
He then went to Wegmans
Bought food
At the checkout he couldn't find his credit cards
The cashier told him
They would put his bags behind the counter
He could come back
He figures he left them at Aldis
They tell him no one has handed in any credit cards
They are not in the car
He checks the parking lot
He goes home and cancels the credit cards
He then remembers
That he had paid earlier for my mothers eye drops
And had thrown them into the grocery bag in Wegmans
So he has to go back to Wegmans for the drops
On getting there
It is unusually quiet at the customer service desk
He tells his story to a women behind the counter
Another women approaches
Asks if these are his bags

He says yes
He asked, on a long shot
Did anyone return credit cards here
They did
Both his cards were returned
They then ask does he want to pay for the groceries
He tells them he has canceled these cards
And then finds that he forgot to bring cash with him
The women he had told his story to
Tells him to try the cards
Maybe it didn't go through yet
Both cards are dead

At that moment
The women who had heard his story
Turned to the women trying to check out my father
She tells her give him the groceries
I am going to pay for them
My father objects
The women processes the groceries and gives my father the bags
He says at least let me pay you back, what's you name
She just smiled
My father reaches out his hand
Says thanks my name is Stan Richmond
She smiles at his attempt to catch her off guard
And tell him her name
She turned around and continued with her work
Now other people were waiting
My father returned home with the groceries
My father sat for a long time thinking about what had happen
She said to him
I have a dad like you

It's Snowing And Cold, May 2011

I am told spring is here
I am told Bin Laden has been killed
I am told don't think about Fukushima
I am told 25 years later Chernobyl is still not over
I am told Kent State happened 40 years ago

I am told there's no money for health care
I am told there is money for war

I am told there's no money for the poor
I am told there is money for Bonuses for the rich

I am told Bank America has no choice
I am told they have to foreclose
I am told don't ask about the billions in bailout

I am told
I am told
I am told a lot of things
While it snows
And I am telling you
I am trying to keep warm

Looking In A Window Of A Cafe

A Man and Woman
Sit at a table
At the window
She has her back to him
She is looking out the window
Forcefully
She seems to be looking at nothing

He looks like he is about to cry
He is looking at the back of her head
His mouth is part open
With a look
Of he doesn't know what to say
It doesn't looked like a happy scene

I hear the food is good there
I was just walking by
Looking in a window of a cafe

The Light Turned Green

Lotto
Beer
Cigarettes
Bread
Milk
Pizza
And the car always needs gas

Our Main Character
Read the words
Written around
The top of the building
They repeated all the way around

The Store
Gas station
Was on a corner
Of two big streets
While sitting at the red light

The parking lot was full
People buying Lotto numbers
Hoping to win
Buying beer and cigarettes
To cushion the loss
One must eat
Bread, Milk and Pizza
And the car always needs gas

Buying Lotto, hoping to win
Buying beer and cigarettes
To cushion the loss
One must eat
Bread, Milk and Pizza
And the car always needs gas

The light turned green
Driving into the horizon

With hopes
That there's got to be more then

Lotto
Beer
Cigarettes
Bread
Milk
Pizza
And the car always needs Gas

Northampton - What About The Artists?

It was 1979
I pulled into Haydenville
In a VW camper
I camped in a friend's driveway
He had told me to come out from Buffalo, NY
That this is where it was all happening
For artists
He had a studio in Florence, MA
This is when the Iron Horse
Was only one little storefront
They had on the wall
May the Arts live
Later musicians would complain
How are the artists suppose to live?
I was performing juggling in the streets
One day, I was informed the International Juggling Festival
Was happening at Hampshire College
I walked into a room of people throwing things in the air
And at each other
I became a professional juggler
Making my living for more than 20 years
I would be apart of many a first nights
And twice at the really big show at the Academy of Music
Where on the stage one could feel and smell in the curtains
All the great acts that had been there
There were many jugglers in the area
Who would meet in Pulaski Park
When the state closed down the mental institution
The audience became more interesting
And the streets seemed sadder
With many wandering around
With no where to go
There were still many affordable studio spaces
This would soon change
As the city became the hip place to be
As Smith College no longer worried about being
The Lesbian Mecca
New restaurants opened and closed

New restaurants opened and closed
And opened
New businesses came and went
And rents kept climbing
Before they did
There was theater in the streets
In abandoned storefronts
Creativity poured into the streets from alleyways
A vanguard movie house opened, coffee houses,
Dancing the night away at Dance Spree
There were hovels known as bars
That gave some of the greatest bands in this area
A crowded sweaty religious experience
That soon would be cleaned up
Made into hip clubs
That lost the edge
Now it would take someone a few weeks
To eat in all the restaurants
Hip shops continue to open
As prices go up
The wandering lost people
Seem to have wandered somewhere else
There is still the street musician, here and there
And those that ask for spare change
And the venues for Known Artists has increased
Where there are a number of shows to be seen on any given night
Yet the up and coming artists have moved out
Getting pushed from one down and out city to another
As the hipness follows and the prices go up
They search for other abandon buildings
Low rent districts, factors that haven't been turned into malls
The sign reads
Let the arts live
What about the artists?

Smoochie Mochie

Yes Smoochie Mochie
I was wondering why I don't have more
Smouchie Mochie
In my life
I decided to go out and look for it
I found others who were interested

With many it was like lighting striking
Then soon there was the thunder
A devastating storm
It had me question
Just what was Smoochie Mochie
And why did I think I needed it

Snow Shovel

It's snowing
A couple of inches now
More on the way
I am here at my parents
Hoping I will be able to drive home tomorrow
One can get stuck in Buffalo
With the lake effect
When no one else has snow
There is tons of it here
I ask my father
Who is 86 years old
Does he have a snow shovel?
He says happily yes
It's on the porch
I look out
There is an old snow shovel
All bent up
Handle about to fall off
Not much of a shovel left
I ask if there are any others
No
He has helped me many times in my life
My father doesn't do much shoveling these days
This shovel reminds me of him
He is old
All bent up
Not much left
When I asked if there was another shovel
When he said no
I agreed, there isn't another one of him

Taken

When I looked into her eyes
I felt lighter
I felt like I was being swept away
Taken
OHHHHHH
How I wanted to be taken

Later in court
Listening to her lawyer
I couldn't see her eyes
She always seemed to be facing the other direction
Head down
Blocked by her lawyer
No I had no regrets

In the drone of the lawyer
Just asking for what is fair
I remember how willingly I went
I cheered
My face was plastered with a smile
Looking into eyes
I felt lighter
I felt swept away
OHHHHHH
How I wanted to be
Taken

I was then informed by the Judge
Just how much I was going to be taken for
I'll always remember her
She had me feeling lighter
I felt swept away
OHHHHHH
How I was
Taken

Big Box Of Happiness

The rain woke me up
When I opened my eyes
The gray light
Reminded me
My empty apartment
My empty fridge
My empty bed
My empty wallet

I remembered the credit card
I found in the parking lot
I am in America
Where
You can buy your happiness
I drag myself down to the nearest
Big box store
I am planning on buy a big box of happiness
When I walk into the store
An employee wearing a costume
Waving me to aisle 7
Happiness is on sale in aisle 7
I run down to aisle 7
I am expecting crowds
Hand to hand combate
Instead I find the Dalai Lama
Standing in front of the pallet
With the last box of happiness
We both stood looking at that box of happiness
The last one
That was on sale
It was just me and the Dalai Lama
It looked like I could take him down with a body check
But then again you never know
Dalai Lama's may have some fancy moves

He didn't seem like he wanted to fight over it
He started talking
I think it had something to do with breathing

Something about the mind
You know focusing the mind
Or maybe it was the other way around
You weren't supposed to focus on anything
And it's everything
I got confused
I realized I am standing next to the Dalia Lama
I should ask him some questions

I asked did he have any good stock tips
I asked could he help me improve my poker game
I asked him if Buddhist had any good pick up lines
He didn't have any answers for my questions
He started to leave
I followed
Looking over my shoulder
At that last box of happiness
I could still run back and get it

In the parking lot
He said he wasn't a religion
We walked our separate ways
I got in my car
Rolled down all the windows
And sat there
No longer feeling empty
Listening to the chanting

Tooth Fairy

What are you trying to tell me
Santa Claus
The guy in the big red suit
He's saying that the Easter Bunny
Isn't real

The leprechauns
The leprechauns are saying
The gold
Isn't real

The wood fairies
The wood fairies are asking
Which reality
Are we talking about

I do admit
That I have some questions
About reality

National Geographic
Said
They have some questions
About the flying reindeer

They need some scientific evidence

Wait Wait
This just in from the Ground Hog
What's he saying
He's saying
It's a crash and burn
He running back to his hole
He's yelling back
It's a crash and burn
It's a crash and burn

Yes I grew up with images
Of burning in Hell
Of course that would be someone else
For I would have the wings
Flying around Heaven

So what are you trying to tell me
That's not going to happen
That's hard for me to accept
Since
I believe in the Tooth Fairy

Near The End

Near the end
Her voice is very low
At times she can't speak at all
Her life force whispers

She can barely walk even with help
Her legs
Just won't

He can't hear
He has hearing aids
His hearing aids are always whistling
The whistling can be heard
Across the room
He doesn't hear it

After a few tries
She says forget it
Her voice is the loudest from frustration
Some how he hears that

He is constantly telling her to speak up
He can't hear
She can't talk
65 years together
It's near the end

Pushing Back and Forth

The scene
A mother
Pushing a child in a stroller
A boy
Getting too big for the stroller
As the mother is walking along
The boy grabs the stroller hood
Above his head
And pushes it back
He stares at his mother
Waiting for a reaction
The moment
There could be a number of reactions
A number of counter reactions

She could slap him
She could slap him
For pushing the hood back
She could yell at him
Don't do that
She could yell at him
While pushing the hood back
And he could push it back again
Escalating the power struggle
The scene could break down here
The mother seemed in a hurry to get somewhere
Now a battle rages on the sidewalk

What actually happen
In this case
The mother smiled
Pushing the hood back
In a playful way
The son pushed it back
The mom smiled again
Pushed it back in a playful way
This game continued
As the mom kept moving

Getting to where she was going
They were both smiling
Playing the game
Of pushing back and forth

Use Titanium

He was five years younger
He loved his older brother
Looked up to him
Wanted his love

When his older brother
Would go out to play
He would spend all day
Building a fort
Working for hours
Creating
An incredible fort with many details
That he wanted to impress
And give to his brother

On his return
The older brother
Would mock his little brother
His response to the fort
Was to destroy it
Kicking the fort
All over the room
Smashing it

40 years later
The older brother
Is still coming by
Looking for forts to smash
Ways to put him down
Creating forts where there aren't any
So that he can smash them

The younger brother
No longer builds forts
For his older brother
He builds them for himself

The older brother hasn't stop trying
To exert his power
He feels powerless
Now that his younger brother
Doesn't want his love

The younger brother
Has at times felt the anger
Of wanting to smash his older brother
For the endless put downs
To destroy him
As he destroyed the forts

On hearing that the older brother
Was coming to visit
His mother
Whom the younger brother lives with
He said he wasn't worried
He had built his present fort
Out of titanium

Money In Different Sizes

The reason
Most were blind
Couldn't see very well
Needed a way to tell the difference
Between bills
So they were made different sizes

The reason
Mustard Gas
Used in World War 1
And homemade booze
Which was so bad
It created blindness
If it didn't kill ya

The War
Had everyone searching
For relief in the booze
Both caused blindness

Business needed to carry on
Money was made different sizes
Customers could keep buying
Regardless if anyone could see
And the Wars rage on

Defending The Elves

Good evening
I am a lawyer with the Law Firm

Justice For The Rich

I am here representing the Elves
Against Santa
For those of you who don't celebrate Christmas
Or who don't believe
You know this is a metaphor anyway

For those of you who had gotten wind
That the Elves were thinking of striking
And disrupting Christmas

Don't worry, the Union for the Elves
Realized to strike on Christmas
Would only bring bad PR
There would be the endless camera shots of crying children
No one would care about the Elves
And the oppressive conditions they have to endure
In the North Pole
Which is melting
Which reminds me of another case
Our firm is working on
In defending the penguins
Who live in the South Pole
Which is melting

The Elves were brought to the North Pole
With promises of jobs and prosperity

The Elves tell a different story
Where they work
Long hours
Making crap
Nothing that really needed
They feel useless

All meaning to life has been lost

When asked about the rumors
Of the Union asking that
The children be removed
They said yes
They didn't want them working
In the same horrible conditions

Other complaints
Are about lack of choices
They have to buy all their supplies
Through the Santa's warehouses
Where prices are high
To help Santa offered
Santa credit cards
With Santa interest

Then there are the Santa mortgages
The Santa Banks
With all this help from Santa
The Elves find themselves
Outside and homeless
Living with the huskies

It may sound familiar
The names have been changed
But those on the bottom
Are getting fucked

I am here to represent them
At least until their pension plan is gone

Then they are on their own

Our law firm has a reputation
We will write every possible appeal
To just keep the case going
Even though we all know it's not going anywhere

We will be dealing with the scab Elves
Making next years toys
Mean while we are taking donations
For the soup kitchens
For the Elves and their families
This is a time to remember what they have done for you
Try not to focus on all the times
You didn't get what you wanted from Santa
It wasn't the Elves fault

The only statement we have from the Santa headquarters
Rape them until they plead guilty

This might sound harsh coming from Santa
But he's got a job to do

This year while opening up your presents from Santa
Remember the Elves

This was sponsored by
Rudolf the whistle-blower

Don't Eat The Yellow Snow
Thanks Frank Zappa

Where are we
We are in Oregon
Out in the woods
Looking at a pristine reservoir

Security cameras
Watching a guy
Stumbling
Down the hill
Through the bushes
Over a fence
And then
Pissing in the reservoir

The guy apologized in court
Said it was stupid
He had been partying
And instead of picking a bush
He pissed in the reservoir

A healthy bladder holds up to 16 ounces of urine
According to the National Institutes of Health

This wasn't a pristine reservoir
This water was
Chlorinated
Pumped into this
Reservoir
For drinking water

They emptied the reservoir
At a costs of more then $45,000
8 million gallons of Chlorinated water

Remembering pissing in a pool
I didn't drink
Pool water

The water bureau stated it's not about the science
16 ounces of urine
In 8 million gallons of chlorinated water
"There's no health risk"
The head of the bureau said
I am dealing with the "yuck factor"
He didn't want to get hundreds of calls
I made orange juice this morning
With that water
And I got sick
He said he didn't want to hear it

I'll tell ya what I don't want to hear

Strontium 90 and Tritium
Being leaked by VT Yankee Nuclear Power Plant
Into the Connecticut River
Does anyone see that as
Yucky
They didn't drain the Connecticut
Or shut down the plant

And when I was growing up in Buffalo, NY
Lake Erie actually burned in the 70's
Chemicals and pollutions so thick
We used to play
I am Jesus
And walked on the water

Where was the water bureau then?

Let's not forget the small creeks
Behind the factories
That all have their lawns cut out front
In the back
Where the steams flow
Depending what they are pouring in
It is a different color
Each day

Where is the yucky factor?
Making that company clean up and stop dumping

In India
Some people drink their own piss for health reasons
It is said the first piss in the morning is the one to drink

If you think this is yucky
You need to get over it
For the next time
You are stranded in a lifeboat
In the middle of the ocean
It is recommended that you drink the piss
Of the other people in the boat
Your own piss contains vitamins that you don't need
Someone else might have the vitamins you are missing
If you are thirsty and want to live
You drink their piss
And not the ocean water

The health reasons given in India
It will prevent colds
The guy who had drank his piss
Had a slight cold
So it doesn't seem to work for everyone

Many of us are still rebelling
From when we were in grade school
Where we had to raise our hands
To get permission
And state whether or not
We had to go number one or number two
Even the idea of telling everyone what you had to do
Restricted many a sphincter

Instead of being a society
That allows you to take a piss when you need to
Instead of roaming around the city
Looking for some place to piss
Getting looks from restaurants owners

Because you are just coming in to piss
Or finding a gas station
With a bathroom that is working
Or that you can walk into
Otherwise you find a corner somewhere
That smells like someone else had to do the same

So the next time your out there and drunk
And need to take a piss
It might be hard to find a place
Where there are no security cameras

So in the adventure of finding a place to piss
All I want to say is
Stop pissing in the water

You Have Such Cold Hands

Oh Baby
Your hands are cold

OHHHHH
No I am not complaining
I just amaze myself
On what I will accept
For love
I know at one time
I said I had some standards
And yes I have to admit
That as I get older
Those standards are loosening
In fact I think there's been a complete break down
In retrospect
The jury is still out
On whether those standards
Were even needed
Should they have been
Broken down
Done away with
Many years ago
Especially in those times
When I was bemoaning being alone
And there were those
With open arms
Wanting me
Is it possible I was waiting around for cupid's arrow?
When really I am cupid

We are all cupid
So who shoots the first arrow?
And when it strikes
Will one feel joy?
Or aggression?
And will the battle begin once more

I thought the movie we are searching for
Was the couple by the fireplace
Just getting in from the cold
Laying near the fire
Snuggled up
Savoring the wine and food
Each other's skin

Ohhhhh baby
Your hands are cold

I Love The Photo

Yes
I love the photo
I mean
I fell in love
With the photo
I mean
I fell in love with the woman
In the photo
I mean
I don't know the woman in the photo

So can I fall in love with her?

Am I falling for an image
I have seen in movie after movie
I mean
Who is she really?
I mean
Why does she look
Like a different woman
In each photo

In this photo
The light shines on her thick hair

I mean
Is it the thickness of her hair
That I imagine
My hands getting tangled in

Or is it her long neck
That she shows
With the tilt of the head
That I want to hold

There are the eyes
There's a look
That she knows I am looking

The cigarette
That dangles
Is a prop
It's in the way
Guarding
Her lips

The look
I am over here
Tangle yourself in my hair
Hold my neck
As you bring your lips to mine

Ohhh
Those eyes
That know
Whether this is a stolen kiss
Or a kiss of devotion

There is a wildness to the whole picture
And the cigarette is the signal
I am out on the town
Looking for some wildness
Let the jungle drums beat loudly

I mean it was just a photo
I mean it was a photo, of a woman I didn't know
I mean why am I hearing the jungle drums
I mean why am I dressing in safari
I mean it's just a photo

I kept looking at it
She is looking at me
All I am trying to say

I just fell in love with a photo

She's Suspicions

He was standing there
With a bouquet of flowers
And two bars of chocolate
Organic Chocolate
Which she loves

Why would he have flowers and chocolate
Unless he had obviously fucked up royally
He of course was not letting on to anything
He was just standing there
With a littler larger then necessary bouquet of flowers
And the chocolate

She thought
Well let's milk this
You know I was feeling a little hungry
He said lets go out to your favorite restaurant
She smiled
She said do you feel that cold breeze in the air
He said may be we should go
To one of the islands in the Caribbean

At this point
She had to know
She said
What happened
What did you do
What are you regretting

He said
I fell in love with you
I am here for you
I don't regret it

She kissed him
She still had her suspicions

Valentine - Cupid

Googling Valentine
A monk
Who was told
Not to marry
Young men and women
By the government at the time

For it was easier
To get the men to fight
If they weren't married

The monk
Valentine
Did it on the side
Married them in secret
And was caught
Put into prison
Wrote love letters
From prison
Was killed
Became know as St Valentine

Cupid
Who is Cupid
A boy armed with bow and arrows
He is also portrayed as a young man with his beloved Psyche
Cupid has always played a role in
The celebrations of love and lovers.

Shooting arrows
And if you are hit
You are in Love
With the next person you meet

Seems hard to believe that there would only be one Cupid
The millions of people who are falling in love
That's a lot of arrows
If there was more then one Cupid

That could be complicated

With all the lonely people
Maybe there is only just one
Over worked
Cupid
Who can't get to everyone

Cupid is usually for people who are single
I wondered
If cupid
Shot an arrow or two
At those in long term relationships

I decided to do a little research
Googling Cupid
Brought up all kinds of sites
I researched thoroughly

I found out about a number of things
That my mother or father hadn't told me about
Or any of those attempts at sex education classes
These web sites
Encouraged more sex
Than most religions would allow

I didn't have much better luck
Contacting the Cupid hot lines

I understand that those who are single
Might get some preference
But if Cupid could find some time in his busy schedule
I would be much appreciative

If there is a foundation
Where I can donate for the cost of arrows
I would be happy too

For It is honorable thing to do
To honor St Valentine

To Stop the wars
To encourage love
To be shot with an arrow
To feel the energy
To know one is alive
Connected

What Can I Say?

What can I say?
What can you hear?
What do you want to hear?
What do I want to tell you?
What do I say to strangers?
What do I announce to everyone
What is said to a chosen few
What is known as a secret
What is never said?
What will be said later?
What could be said?
What was said before?
What others hoped you would say
What you wished you had said
What you wished you had never said
What you thought you said
What you had said to the wrong person
What was said, that you didn't want to hear
What can I say?

Don't say it on Tuesdays
That's all I have to say
Don't say it on Tuesdays

I hope that was helpful?

Watch This

She is 86
She walks over with her walker
She sits on the chair
She say
Watch this
She moves herself to the edge of the chair
She says
It's important to have your poopy
She is pointing to her ass
On the edge of the chair
Then she grabs the walker
And lifts herself up
She said see that
And she sits again
Saying again
The key to the maneuver
Is having the poopy
On the edge of the chair

She was showing me this
Because I had said my mom was 90
Having a hard time getting out of a chair
She was showing concern
A helpful hint
The third time she was showing me
She was having a hard time herself
She was getting tired

There is a time when
No maneuver will help
The body just isn't doing it any more
No one likes to be there
There is the hope
That one could get better
But the reality is that your body
Gets old
Doesn't work any more

She is sitting in a chair
Lifting up her leg
Holding it there for a few seconds
Proud of herself that she is doing
Her exercises

In a few moments
She stops
Looks at me
Looks to see if anyone else is listening
Leans towards me
She says
I am getting sick of it
I am ready to go

Her Biggest Fear

The relatives informed the police
Her greatest fear
Was that she would burn to death
Lose her life in a fire

She lived a life of fear and struggle
She died and was buried
A few days later
Her grave was dug up
Randomly from the new burials in the graveyard
By an ex-convict
Scheming an insurance fraud
Her body was taken
Put in a car
Drench with lighter fluid
Ignited

Pushed off the cliff
To simulate a car crash
Where the car and driver
Were burned beyond recognition
Then the insurance was going to be collected
By the girl friend
Then both would run off to Mexico

They were caught

The women who lived a life
Of fear and disappointments
Had made it to her grave
Avoiding her worse fear
Only to be dragged from her grave
For one last disappointment

Self Awareness Section

Welcome to
Them R Us
I am your personal guide
Who will be taking you
Through our store
Giving a personal touch
To the fleecing

Them R Us
Is part of the corporate division
This is good for Us
Translated by Them
It's Good For You

As we walk through the store
You will notice some familiar items

There have been some changes
We can honestly say that everything is made in USA
With Right To Work Law Legislation
It is now cheaper to out source to America

We have made the shopping carts bigger
You can pile in even more crap that you don't need

Yes we are a All in one store
We have everything you can imagine
Except the basics needs

We have also added a few new sections
And one very hard to find section
And you look like someone who
Might be interested in going there
I can help you avoid the BS
Involved in finding this section
So follow me

Let's just walk around this crowd
Fighting over the new phones
We actually have more in the back

As you can see the store stretches
In every direction as far as the eye can see
We are going to the back of the store
Past the
Alcohol
And Pharmaceuticals
And the Lingerie
Where I some times get lost

But just past there
Is our new section
It is a self-awareness section

Here at
Them R Us
We respond to demand
With all the contradiction and lies
The demand for answers continues to rise
Where's there demand
There is money to be made
At Them R Us
You will notice that the shelves are filled
With everything you need for self-awareness

We have holy robes in any color
You can get a 5 pack with one of each color
We have incense made from
Every holy ghetto we could find

Take for example
Our organic sage
Which we have in small hand made pouches
For ceremonies and purification
We also have sage in bales
Along with Industrial incense burners
For big jobs

Like purifying congress

We have
Yoga classes
Along with all the latest yoga accessories
Meditation pillows
Primal therapy books on cd
An Astrology section
Tarot Decks
The I Ching
Tea leaves and the tea cups in sets of 12
Crystal balls
Those that light up in the dark
One that can be used as a lava lamp in off hours
We have books on
How to create your own self-awareness business
We have some Mayan calendars that are out of date
We just about have it all
All the accessories and chachkies you'll ever need
You name it
It's here
In the self-awareness section

You can request a sitting with a guru
One of our employees will dress the part
Sit in front of this mountain backdrop
And answer your questions
On my shift as guru, I prefer to be myself
And tell you ahead of time
I don't have the answers

Let me warn you
Many who become self aware
Realize how depressed they are
We do offer some coupons for the pharmacy department

Some have asked us about the spiritual drugs
What some consider consciousness raising drugs
Does Them R Us carry Weed or LSD
At the moment Them R Us does not

But when we do
You will be able to get the large family pack
For the time being
You can meet me in the parking lot on my break
And I will see what I can do

Between you and me
I find everything about this symbolic
You wade through
The frenzy of buying
For the sake of buying
Past all the plastic and junk one doesn't need
Without help from a kind soul
You could wander around aimlessly
Visiting the same sections over and over
Like our liquor store
Which does have some good prices
Try to avoid the free samples in the pharmaceutical section
And yes those tempting illusions in the lingerie section
But even if you reached the self-awareness section
Most get lost in all the accessories

For those of us who work here
Between you and me
It's a bad joke
We work for low pay
Not enough for housing
Needing food-stamps to eat
Many of us live in the parking lot
In our broken down cars
Have no benefits
We can't afford anything in
The self-awareness section

Them R Us makes all this possible
At a price
That will not sustain life on the planet

Any Questions?

Searching

He looked into her eyes

Deeply

She said
What you are searching for
You're not going to find

Looking
In my eyes

In The Good Old Days

In the good old days
When you body was just left out back
And your dog would find your bones

In the good old days
When you could just dump shit out the back window
Off the back porch
And then wondered why the dog died

In the good old days
When you could
Go down to your neighbor's house
And burn it
Take their wife
Shoot their dog

In the good old days
When you dropped bombs
To find out what would happen
And more than the dog died

In the good old days
When you made chemicals
That could kill anything
And you sprayed it on everything

In the good old days
When you dumped
Anything you wanted
Into the water
It changed color
Bubbled up and boiled
Caught on Fire
Fish floating on top
A toxic cocktail

Let's drink a toast
To future generations

Trying to find clear water

In the good old days
When you picked someone out
By their nationality
By how they looked
By who they prayed to
How they defined themselves sexually
By the color of their skin
The list goes on and on
Giving reason
To hunt them down
To exterminate them

There is something wrong with
Saying they were the good old days
Is it because the future seems even scarier
To be able to look back fondly
On the times
With friends, family, being in the world
With time passing
One looks back fondly
In the good old days

Do your part
Now
To have a past
That one can really say
In the good old days

What Did I Just See

Walking back from the compost pile
Suddenly saying to myself
I am not being present
I am off
On automatic pilot
In my mind saying this and that
This is all in a reaction to a phone call
I had just hung up from
What I would say now
What I will say in the future
Running many different scenarios
Suddenly I stop
Tell myself to take a breath
I look up into the sky

I catch a bird out of the corner of my eye
Then there are 7 of them in formation
No there is one more
Flying alone
But to the outside of the formation

Was that bird on the outside
Just late
Was it catching up
It didn't look like it was trying to be in the formation
It was flying along
But on the outside
Had this bird been thrown out
Now flying to the outside
Hoping to get back in
Maybe this bird was the one
Giving directions to the others in the formation

Was this one of those Cosmic snapshots
Showing the collective working together
Along with a strong individual
Wasn't this some sign for me to interrupt

When I brought myself to the present
I saw birds in a formation
And
One bird flying alone

That's what I saw

More Material

This is ancient story
In fact this story is so old
It's before we had anthropologists

It's about a tribe in the jungle
Who were surrounded by Lions

Everyday the Lions would attack
Everyday the tribe would fight back
Everyday there would be
Casualties

The tribe talked about this endlessly
What could they do?
They had killed many Lions
Yet
More Lions kept coming

One day one of the members of the tribe
Came forward
And announced he had an idea
He was a poet
No one in the tribe liked poetry
And poets even less

He had an idea
And since no one else did
They agreed to listen
To his idea
As long as he didn't
Tell it to them
As a poem

The poet said
I think I know how to soothe the lions

Everyone was listening
The poet said

Poetry saved my life
Each poem
Was received as a gift
He wanted to share this gift
With the Lions
He was sure
Poetry
Would soothe them
Stop them from attacking

He was offering to the tribe
That he would go out
And read his poems to the Lions
For the safety of the tribe

Everyone was happy to send out the poet
They even packed him a lunch
For they all had heard
His poems too many times

So the poet
Wandered out
Looking for the best place
To have his reading
Wanting to have
The right atmosphere

Our poet found a place
And waited for the Lions
Lions started to arrive
The poet waited
As long as he could
To fill up some of the empty seats

Once our poet was surrounded
Our poet started reciting his poetry
The Lions began to relax
They were soon sitting down
Enjoying the sun
And listening to our poet

Back in the village
The tribe saw no signs of Lions
Could it be possible?
The poet was soothing the Lions

A whole day came and went
With no Lions attacking
People were now talking about
The value of poetry and Poets
And argued about what the poems meant

Back at the reading
The Lions were relaxed
As long as the poet read
When the poet stopped
The Lions would become
Agitated
And move closer

Our poet tried to repeat a poem
Which also made the Lions
Agitated
Our poet was coming to the end
Of the poems he had with him
As he approached the last poem
He was drawing a blank
To try and make up new poems
On the spot

The Lions ate the poet
Once he ran out of poems
And they were even more content
A few days had passed
The villagers were grateful to the poet
Everyone had a new appreciation for poetry
And they all agreed
The next poet
Would have to have

More material

The Look

I walked into a room
I looked around
I was looking for someone
I found her
I was staring
When she looked my way
She looked away
She looked back
I was still looking
She has seen that look before
She looked down
She looked up

She looked up
As if to verify
Yeah he's got the look

He then watched
Her partner snuggle up to her
Whisper something into her ear
He watched as she laughed
Her mouth
Her head titled back

He continued to look around
Scanning the crowd
Most seemed taken
He then noticed
Someone looking at him
He looked away
To make it look
Like he was looking for someone
Well he was
He looked back
They were still looking
They had the look

Let the Negotiations Begin

What is it that you have?
How badly do I want it?
How badly do I need it?
Am I thinking clearly?

Do I see that I have choices?

What is it that you have?
How badly do I want it?
How badly do I need it?

Let the Negotiations Begin

It Occurred To Me

I was given a
Lottery ticket
As a gift
Never looked at it
Don't remember where I put it
It was never claimed
It was announced that the winning ticket
Was never claimed

She sat across from me in school
I would always sneak glances
At times I would just stare
Never talked to her
At the 40th reunion
She told me she was madly in Love with me
Thought of me for years after we graduated
Thought I wasn't interested

I was told to show up for a job interview
I didn't go
Felt I didn't have a chance
After many years of shit jobs and no money
Panhandling in the streets
A successful looking guy
Throws me some money
Asked if I remember him
Tells me the interview was just a formality
The job was mine if I had showed up

I wanted to sing
I never sang
I tried out for the chorus
I was told to practice a song
I went home
I sang it to myself
I never sang it out loud
I didn't sing in the chorus

I sit with a the group of people
Waiting for the workshop
To start
The workshop leader
Finally arrives
Says welcome to
How not to be a loser
Before we start
Some logistics need be dealt with
I was informed
That I haven't filled out the paper work
Correctly
That I wouldn't be able to take the workshop
How not to be a loser
I was asked to leave
As everyone else watched me
Walk out
It occurs to me
I might be a loser

Now I Know

There are some of us
Who grew up
With a TV show
Of a bare chested white guy
Bounding his fists on his chest
And making this sound
AHHHHHHahahhhahahhh

Tarzan
Any way I found this Tarzan movie
In a friend's drawer I was looking through
While house sitting
I was just checking
To see how the under garments were folded
When I found this movie
This was one of those Tarzan movies
That wasn't seen on TV
This is before porn on the internet
You had to go to one of those video stores
That had a back-room
It seemed those who wanted those videos
Always seemed to know where to find them
It was never advertised
Some friends told me about it

This back-room had
TV show take offs
There was one of Bewitched
Where she wrinkled her nose
And there were a number of sculptured men
And Women
Waiting her command

Being a fan of Tarzan
And wanting to know more about this friend
I was house sitting for
I watched the movie
The story was basically

Jane gets tired of waiting around for Tarzan
Who was always swinging off
It shows Jane listening to
All those jungle sounds
The drumming from the near by village
This throws Jane into a frenzy
She didn't leave Tarzan a note
He doesn't read

You see Jane running through the jungle
Where she first encounters a passing safari
There was always a safari going by
She devours the safari sexually
Leaving the Bwanas and their native carriers
Naked and scattered through out the jungle
She continues on towards the drumming
Where she stays for a few days
Having sex with every
Available
Man and Woman
In the tribe

Tarzan returned
To find Cheetah
Standing in the corner
With his hands over his eyes

Tarzan called out
But there was no sign of Jane
When she came back
She found Tarzan distraught
Wondering what had happen
Wanting to know why the bwanas
Kept asking for her
Jane told Tarzan everything
Down to the last moan
Tarzan was speechless
Though Tarzan didn't talk much anyway
Jane said
It feels so good to get that out of my system

She then looked around the hut
And asked Tarzan what was for supper
Since she was quite hungry

The next scene is Tarzan
Beating his chest and making those sounds
Ahhhhh ahhhhhhh ahhhhhh
As this story ends
It implies this is why
Tarzan beats his chest
Making those awful noises
Calling out to all who can hear
On the TV show it would show Tarzan doing this
And always showed all the animals running and hiding

I always wondered what it meant for Tarzan
To beat his chest and make those sounds
Now I know

I Need The Money

Sitting in an outdoor cafe
She approached my table
She said I am a fortune-teller
You need not say anything

She sat down

First
I can see you are a little hesitant
About the price

How do I know this?

I am fortune-teller after all

I can tell you
Since I can see the future
And I am a hypnotist
That when I leave
You will be thinking to yourself
I should have of paid more
I should have of paid more
I should have of paid more

Now lets get down to what's on your mind
No don't tell me
I am a fortune-teller after all
You want to know when you will meet the love of your life
No
You want to know when you will become famous
No
You want to know when your fortune will arrive
No
Then what do you want to know?
I thought you would know
Being a fortune-teller
You would tell me something I needed to know

The fortune-teller said
The sky is blue sometimes
We all need oxygen
I need the money

Homeless

Authorities in a city
Have cleared out
"The Jungle"
It is called the Jungle
In every city
It was reported as one of the largest
Homeless encampments
In the nation
There are larger ones
This one had 300 people living there
The people interviewed
Said it like a big family
We look out for each other
Especially the single females
We checked in on each other
We were all we had

The city decided to clear the area
Stating that there were increasing
Security issues
Public health issues
Pollution issues
There were a lot of issues
And winter was coming on

They said they put 140 people
In shelters, hotels and motels
Others were given rent subsidies
But haven't found places to live
It was said that not all the Jungle residents
Could count on the city to place them in homes
As the city only budgeted
10 million dollars

4 million has already been spent
Trying to keep people out

Why piss it way
Paying for hotels
That only temporarily provide housing
Until the money runs out
People are homeless again
With no jobs

10 million dollars
300 people
Why not build sustainable small housing
For all of them
With plenty of money left over
For job training
Health Care
Transportation
With still plenty
Of money
For those who take their cut
To grease palms
And buy elections

Mean while
More money is being spent
To install reinforced fencing
To keep people out

Where do we want the homeless to go?

Do we really want to solve the problem?

Pep Talk

The word on the street is
We're Fucked

The daily propaganda
Nothing is going to change

The mantra everyone repeats
It's useless to try

It's a lie
It's a lie

Things happen
Because you make them happen
You can't just ask for them
You try to make them happen

There is mounting evidence
By the military personal and vehicles
That are surrounding us
That this is not going to be a party

It has been proven
Most of the news
Is a distraction and false

I am afraid to break it to you all
That it is much worse than reported

Now is no time for despair

Even if all the means
Have been deployed to destroy
Us
You would be amazed
At our abilities
To survive

I know many of you are wondering
Just what is the catch
How much is all this going to cost
It always comes down to that

It is obvious
That it is way more then we bargain for
There are no sales
And even at the lowest price
The price is too high

It has been scientific proven
Depending on my hunger
I will eat anything

Which God
To pray to
Don't all of them
Have the message of love
Compassion
Helping those who are down
Seems to fall on deaf ears
As the killings continue

Now that we gathered around the collection plate
Many of you are asking
How much should I give
If you are asking me
I say for future generaltions

Give it everything you Got
Give it everything you Got

Can't Wait For Summer

It looks like spring
Except it is 18 degrees
No snow
Doing yard chores
If I think about tasting tomatoes
The summer I love
Will already be over
Focus on collecting the maple syrup

The Best Friend

You might want to ask
Your best friend
Why she was here
Naked
In our house
While you were away

When I asked
She said
She always thought of me as a caring person
Someone who would make a good Doctor
That is why she was spreading the sheet
Over the kitchen table
As she climbed on top
She said
I need
A complete examination
Doctor

Rocks

My distant relatives
In Poland
Were seen standing in their fields
Throwing rocks at Tanks

Polacks, talk funny
"Throw the horse over the fence some hay"

Throwing rocks at tanks
Didn't stop the tanks

Hundreds of Palestinian children
Were put into prison
For throwing rocks
At Israeli civilians and soldiers
Others were killed

Young boys throw rocks at each other
At cars
At windows
Johnny
How many times have I told you
Don't throw rocks

What is the point of throwing rocks?

When you are under siege
My relatives wouldn't go down
Without a fight
Only having rocks as weapons

Here comes my best shot

Let's Be Clear

I think it's important to say this
About that
Other wise
You will think
We are talking about that
And I want to be perfectly clear
About this
It's important
Not to talk about that
Other wise the conversation is confusing
And it doesn't have to be
With communication
We can be on the same page
Following along word for word
Right to the cliff-hanging ending
Where It becomes clear
What this is all about

The Pope & The Dog

The Dog said
To the Pope
I hump anything
I can rub up against
I can lick between my legs
The Pope said
What's your point
The Dog said
I don't see that there is any difference
Between the two of us

The Pope said you are wrong
You are faithful
We are not
You love unconditionally
We do not
You follow your instincts
We create laws
You howl at the full moon
We see our insignificance
In the night sky
Scared
We create Gods

The Dog laughed and said
I like to chase sticks
It seems to make you happy
Especially when I am wagging
My tail
Between you and me
The reason I am wagging my tail
Is that I am really glad
That I am not you

The Pope said
Pray for us

If You're Going To Remember Anything

If you're going to remember anything

That's if you can remember anything

You'll want to remember this

A Women and her son
Are standing in their driveway
There's a snake
In the driveway
The Women
Throws gas on the snake
Tells her son to throw a match
The burning snake goes into the bushes
The bushes start on fire
The burning bushes
Starts the house on fire
The whole house burns down
The snake gets away

If you are going to remember anything

Don't try to Burn
The Snake

Who's Your Captain

Ladies and Gentlemen
This is your captain speaking

Some passages below deck
Have been asking
Why are they standing
Ankle deep in water

The first Official statement
We're doing a deep soaking of the rugs
A thorough cleaning
Sorry for any inconvenience
Nothing to worry about
Go back to your room

Now that the water is
Lapping at your thigh
The lights have gone out
The ship seems to be on it's side
Many of you are doubting
The official explanation's
That everything is ok

In your hearts you know
That everything is not ok

As your captain
I just want to remind you
That it is my job
To tell you
Everything is ok
Everything is ok

As a humanitarian
I feel compelled to say
Unofficially
I would suggestion swimming attire
Once in the water

Look for anything that is floating
To hold on to
I know a lifeboat would be nice
But there were budget cuts
Life boats for economy class
Were the first to go

Actually lifeboats for everyone
Is rarely the reality

As your captain
I want you to know
I am aware that the boat is on it's side
For that very reason I am going to shore
In one of the life boats reserved for me
I can guarantee
That everything
Is going to be ok
As soon
As I get ashore

I will talk to our company experts
Who know
How to present the facts
So that it is obvious to any jury
That it was the passenger's fault

As your captain
I can assure you
Everything is being done
To protect the investors

Counter to the Official statement
That everyone has returned to their rooms
Waiting further instructions

Many have fought their way to the main deck
Some found life jackets
They all jumped off the ship

For those waiting in your rooms
Please remain calm
Practice holding your breath
And await further instructions

The Story Survived

She was pregnant
In a concentration camp
The guards came in one day
Said all pregnant women should line up
That they were going to be offered
Twice the food

She was starving
Something held her back
She felt it was her died parents
Others felt it was God
She didn't get noticed
She didn't go

It turned out
They marched all those women
To the gas chambers
They all died

She survived
And
Her husband
Survived

Their story survived

Garlic Festival

Welcome to the Festival that Stinks

Do you Smell it
I love Garlic
I love the Smell

And If I was to pick
Things that I don't like the smell of
It wouldn't be garlic

I don't know how well you smell things
I smell everything

Well I don't smell everything
I didn't smell Chernobyl
I don't smell Fukashima

Some smells you never forget
Being around bodies
Natural Disasters, Wars
You never forget the smell

Then there are the everyday smells
The bathroom smells
The kitchen smells
The smell of a lover
Before and after making love
The smells of the garden
Smells of a fire burning
Smell of rotten food

It's in the air
The smell of a skunk
The smell that we have to run

Do you smell the Tar Sands
Do you smell the Fracking chemicals
Do you smell the GMOs

Do you smell the bullshit called congress
Now there's a smell
Shutting down the government
Over health care
While spending trillions on the military

Corporations get tax breaks
Record profits

The constant wars
The lies
Of why they are necessary

While shutting down
All programs for the poor
Women and Children

It Smells

I don't really like how it smells
I know
Its not all suppose to smell like roses
But at this rate we may never smell roses again

I don't know about you

I don't really like how it smells

I don't really like how it smells

Give me some organic garlic any day

Save Grandma

Grandma took me out to the swamps
Where Grandpa had gone missing
Mysteriously
Just a few days before

She came out to these swamps
On a regular basis
To catch frogs
For her famous
Frog casserole

We arrived at a spot where she said
We needed to wait
Suddenly a frog
Leaped out of the water
And attached itself
To my bare leg

I scream and grandma
Told me to be quiet
As we watched it grow
With each gulp of my blood

When it got to the size
Grandma wanted
She clubbed it off
And put it in her basket

I looked on in disbelief
As this happen a few times
She explained these are Blood sucking frogs
Not many people liked them
They were her secret ingredient
In her frog casserole
Her casserole was my favorite
At least up to this moment
Now Grandma and blood sucking fogs
Were one

She was all upset
Since a few miles away
They were building one of those big Malls
That would be abandon a few years later
There were laws to stop anyone building on wet lands
The mall was being built on the wet lands
Where the frogs gathered

Building the mall on the wet lands
Some estimated hundreds' of thousands
Possibly millions of frogs would be killed
The scientist concluded
Compete extinction
Since this was their mating habitat
Grandma wanted me to fight the mall
Demand that we save the blood sucking frogs
I explained to grandma most people only want
To save
Dolphins
Cute seals
Or the majestic
Whales and elephants

She was very distraught
What would life be
Without the social picnics
And the frog casserole contests
Which she won regularly
And Harold the farmer down the road
Who said he loved her frog casserole
Grandma pleaded
Save the blood sucking frogs

After brainstorming ideas
I created a marketing campaign
Blood Sucking Frogs
Are cute
No body bought that

Having them as pets
Was disastrous

Showing them playing
And sucking blood
Started a killing frenzy

The key I realized
Is having people eat
Grandma's casserole
Very few wanted to try it
I guess it's one of those things
If you haven't grown up eating it
You think it's weird
For me it was Grandma
Holding the casserole dish
With her big smile
Feeling the Grandma love
Maybe if we all thought of it as
Saving grandma
We could save the blood sucking frogs

These Poems had been published before

Northampton - What about the Artists?

Published 2014 Paradise Found - A Walking and Biking Tour of Northampton, Massachusetts through Poetry and Art by Levellers Press Amherst, MA

It's Snowing and Cold, May 2011

Naugatuck River Review - A journal of narrative poetry that sings Winter 2012 Issue 7 - Contest Issue

Taken

Silkworm 5 - The annual review of the Florence Poets Society 2011

Not Impressed

Di-verse-city 2013 Austin International Poetry Festival Anthology

Saving Grandma

The Greenfield Recorder, April 24, 2015

"Paul Richmond is a fascinating poet - his words are evocative & meaningful. He writes about contemporary issues, about love, about relationships & always with the fine hand of a brilliant observer of the human condition. His readings of his poems are mind-blowing - there's never any doubt in the mind of his audience that he's not only a distinguished poet but also a talented actor who gives life to his words, whether on the printed page or if he's declaiming on stage. I have the good fortune to live in the Pioneer Valley of western Massachusetts. That's where Paul gives readings, hosts regular "Open Mics" and also plans & brings to fruition many, many opportunities for other writers to share their work."

Three previously published books by Paul Richmond

No Guarantees - Adjust & Continue
Living In The Break Down Lane - Ready or Not
Too Much of a Good Thing - In the Land of Scarcity -
Breeds Contempt
new book
The 24 Hour Store Was Closed

Human Error Publishing:
www.humanerrorpublishing.com
Monthly readings
Annual events
Publishing other authors
The Greenfield Annual Word Festival www.gawfest.org
The Garlic & Arts Festival Word Stage   http://garlicandarts.org

Reviews

"I looked at a lot of your fabulous work just now and just wanted to say thanks, loved it, brilliant of course, and hilarious, not to mention that it's great satire. Sometimes reminded me of Laurie Anderson's United States, in that league. Sure you've heard all this before, just wanted to add my vote, and say thank you!"

Avant Guard Dog Studios Marc D'avegan Rubin

"Paul Richmond is a poet, performer and assassin of apathy that I met back in Austin in 2010 and he just provided me with his youtube channel. He constantly bombs me with encouragement to get over my angst and just be awesome and create like him.
Everyone should collectively check him out
http://www.humanerrorpublishing.com

Brent Downes - Feature Author at Trimass International Publishers

My dream, my desire, my lust and hunger is to spend two hours writing thank you notes. After 16 minutes, you're up. What a guy! Holy cow! Holy catfish! Holy mother of the ancient deep fat fried pickle sandwich! You are a piece of work and I love you! Thank you 10,000 times. I will not number each one individually, but you get the point I hope.
Thank you, beloved captain of my sinking ship, beloved dog explaining me to a bar tender, beloved Paul Richmond. People loved you and you sold 40 books!! YEE HA!!

Pat Jobe - Minster - Nice Folks at Greenville Unitarian Universalist Fellowship, SC

www.ingramcontent.com/pod-product-compliance
Lightning Source LLC
Chambersburg PA
CBHW071156090426
42736CB00012B/2352